Papa's Little Princess

by CARROLL BONNER

Papa's Little Princess
Copyright © 2020
Carroll Bonner

All rights reserved. Printed in the United States of America. No part of this book may be reproduced in any manner whatsoever without written permission except in the case of brief quotations embodied in critical articles or reviews.

Scripture taken from the HOLY BIBLE, KJV and The Message Versions.

ISBN: 978-0-9890787-5-7
Printed in the United States of America

Printing Number
10 9 8 7 6 5 4 3 2 1

Printed by Rocky Heights Print and Binding

THE COVER PICTURE
The Author
Carroll Bonner

Carroll Bonner has turned past life experiences into messages and sermons to reach women of various age, race, religion, and social statuses. She is a native of Selma, Alabama, and the youngest of seven children born to her truly amazing mother, Martha Walton. All admire that Carroll, also known as Lady Bonner, is happily married to Bishop Patrick Bonner, Sr., who serves as overseer of Potter's Place Church, Selma, Alabama. She is the proud mother of Destini and Patrick Jr., who both serve in ministry at Potter's Place. Lady Bonner is a born-again believer who has been called by God and uses her obedience to God's calling mostly by encouraging ladies in their healing, self-esteem, purpose, and walk with God. She is passionate about her founded ministry entitled

"Sending for the Women,"

inspired from Jer 9:17 (NIV)
This is what the LORD Almighty says: "Consider now!
Call for the wailing women to come; send for the most skillful of them.

She is also designer of the LG Collection: LETTING GOD, LIFTING GOD, LIVING GOD and LOVING GOD printed on various fabrics and worn by many. Her most recent vision and accomplishment was the start of a program called "Girls with Pearls". Its purpose is to inspire little girls and help develop and motivate them in basic social and behavioral skills.

More so, Lady Bonner is also loved and venerated by many for her charisma, intelligence, and gentle heart. She loves the word of God and has taken deeply to

Galatians 2:20 (KJV)

"I am crucified with Christ, nevertheless I live, not I but the Christ that liveth in me. The life that I now live is of the faith of the son of God who love me and gave himself for me."

Dedication

This book is dedicated to my beautiful daughter, Destini Bonner, my inquisitive little granddaughter, Erinn K Smith, and little Payten Grace Bonner, my youngest granddaughter. It's my prayer the principles and instructions given in this book will be shared with the generations to come.

Foreword

I am sure there are many instructions written to guardians and parents concerning the assignment of raising children, yet parenting is only effective if the child can understand life and purpose on their level.

Many children are not building relationships with God until much later in age, and by then they are usually unprepared to weather the storms of life. I encourage Moms, Dads, Guardians, and Teachers to share the information from this book with little girls throughout the world.

Contents

Chapter 1 .... God's Introduction

Chapter 2 .... Map

Chapter 3 .... Parents and Guardians

Chapter 4 .... Prayer Time

Chapter 5 .... The Girl in the Mirror

Chapter 6 .... Play Time

Scriptures noted in KJV and The Message versions

Princess–
Place Your Picture Here

Princess–
Place Your Family Picture Here

CHAPTER 1
God's Introduction

Hi Moms, Dads, Guardians, and Teachers,

I am so happy you chose this book for your little girl. The very first challenge for you is to help your little one to know who our God is. He existed before the beginning of the earth. She also needs to understand God's role in all of our lives, including the kind of miracles He is able to perform. Help her understand His pure love for us and how He is omnipresent, meaning everywhere at the same time. The messages to your little Princess will be as if God is speaking to her. He has inspired me to write to her and give understanding of why it is important to recognize our Creator. Remember to use the scripture references when talking to her about Him. As she grows older, these words will grow in her spirit.

Hi Little Princess,

I am your Father and your God. Please do not be afraid to listen to me. I created all humans and everything you see around you.

Genesis 1:1-2

The Message (MSG)
Heaven and Earth Creation
First this: God created the Heavens and Earth—all you see, all you don't see. Earth was a soup of nothingness, a bottomless emptiness, an inky blackness. God's Spirit brooded like a bird above the watery abyss.

I know everything, and I am everywhere. I can even see everything, and even though you do not see me, I am with you all the time. Don't cry or worry about dolls and other pretty things. I will supply the things you need through the people around you.

Hebrews 13:5-6

The Message (MSG)
Don't be obsessed with getting more material things. Be relaxed with what you have. Since God assured us, "I'll never let you down, never walk off and leave you," we can boldly quote,

God is there, ready to help;
I'm fearless no matter what.
Who or what can get to me?

I really want you to know all about Me, and not exhibit so much excitement about toys and clothes. The more you learn of Me and My will for your life, the better it will be to live on the earth where you are. One day, as you grow older, you will find how important it is to have Me as your heavenly Father. The world down there is torture without Me. People and religion are not gracious like I am. Life as my child will be so much easier.

Matthew 11:29-30

The Message (MSG)

"Are you tired? Worn out? Burned out on religion? Come to me. Get away with me and you'll recover your life. I'll show you how to take a real rest. Walk with me and work with me—watch how I do it. Learn the unforced rhythms of grace. I won't lay anything heavy or ill-fitting on you. Keep company with me and you'll learn to live freely and lightly."

My Princess, this may sound a little funny or unusual, but I live in heaven, high above the clouds in the sky, yet I am still everywhere at the same time. The place called heaven is a very beautiful, and I hope you and your family choose Me as your Savior and Lord. One day you will all live here with Me and the angels.

Mark 13:26-27

"At that time people will see the Son of Man coming in clouds with great power and glory. And he will send his angels and gather his elect from the four winds, from the ends of the earth to the ends of the heavens."

My Father, my God, spoke to me,
A voice so clear and strong.
He said to me, I'm everywhere,
Papa's Princess,
Just know you're never alone.

~CB

Psalm 121:1

I will lift up mine eyes unto the hills, from whence cometh my help.

CHAPTER 2
Map

Hi Moms, Dads, Guardians, and Teachers

I am sure you feel great knowing your little girl now knows of our awesome God! Now the challenge is to really inspire her about the value of the Word of God. Most children today are focused on phones with YouTube and other technologies with all the cartoons, but your challenge is to help them refocus on what God is saying in His word. We have many *new, powerful evils and distractions* in the world today.

Teaching children the Bible and giving them a love for God early on is a matter of life and death. I mean this literally; this learning is a matter of eternal life or eternal death! Remember to use the scripture references in each chapter and other Bible verses to explain the Word of God and His love to her every chance you get.

Hello My Little Princess,

I inspired men to write what I wanted you to know about Me and My heavenly home, so you can get to know me better. Even though they sat down and wrote these words a long time ago, they were not their thoughts. I am the one who inspired them to write the scriptures, so you can know Me and know how to live in this land. What this means is that I really want you to believe in the scriptures and cherish the words in the Holy Bible. This is the Map, or instructions, to live by every day.

2 Timothy 3:16-17

All Scripture is God-breathed and is useful for teaching, rebuking, correcting and training in righteousness, so that the servant of God may be thoroughly equipped for every good work.

Be sure to think on what My Word says all the time, so it is understood. Make sure that you live so others will know that you are My daughter. Trust Me, your lifestyle of good behavior will tell the world whose you are. Please tell your friends about Me so you all can grow together in My Holy Word.

2 Timothy 2:15

Do your best to present yourself to God as one approved, a worker who does not need to be ashamed and who correctly handles the word of truth.

Don't get upset when the word is not saying what you want it to say. If you do not love My Word, then you will look for those who will say what you want to hear and love them more than Me.

2 Timothy 4:3-4

For the time will come when people will not put up with sound doctrine. Instead, to suit their own desires, they will gather around them a great number of teachers to say what their itching ears want to hear. They will turn their ears away from the truth and turn aside to myths.

My dear, as you learn the Bible, you will see in the Word that I have many names. One I'm called is "The Word." Can you guess why this is one of my names?

John 1:1

In the beginning was the Word,
and the Word was with God,
and the Word was God.

Wow! Did you get it right? It is because I am the one who decided what was to be written in the Holy Bible remember? Also, I am the first of everything, including the existence of the word. YES! I AM THE WORD.

If you're listening to the WORD,
Jesus is the voice you heard.
So listen to Him every single day.
It's your map to show you the way.

Hi Princess—

Today you should receive your New Bible!
Write your favorite Bible verse here.

CHAPTER 3
Parents and Guardians

Hi Moms, Dads, Guardians, and Teachers,

I was concerned about you as this portion was being written. It is so hard to help our babies understand they must obey you in the Lord. This puts a responsibility on you to continue learning the Word for your life and for your children. No child can just know God. You are responsible for training and directing them on the right path. This is why most actions from a child are considered the responsibility of the parent. How their behavior is presented usually stems from what they have been allowed to know. Therefore, parents and guardians should really think before allowing children to learn the world's way and not God's way.

Acts 8:31

"How can I," he said, "unless someone explains it to me?"
So he invited Philip to come up and sit with him.

Children must be guided by your life demonstration first, then the voice of authority with love will lead them. They cannot be led effectively by you if you are not an example before them. The experiences and surroundings the children have become their culture. Once some of these bad ways are learned, it becomes hard to change the pattern. It can be changed, but is more difficult than if it were not there. You must earn the respect of children.

Little Princess,

You also have an earthly mother and father or guardians who will teach you lots of things, right? I want them to especially teach about Me and train you about how I want you to live. Always remember that you should be growing closer to Me every day by understanding my Word.

Proverbs 22:6

*Start children off on the way they should go,
and even when they are old they will not turn from it.*

Please obey your parents in the Lord. There will certainly be lots of things that will cause you to not want to obey. This is considered rebellion, and most people do not want to be merciful or gracious to a child who is disobedient. God was so serious about obeying parents, that if you honor them, you will live longer.

Ephesians 6:2

*"Honor your father and mother"
—which is the first commandment with a promise.*

Let me tell you a little about guardians who have been appointed or anointed by God to care for you. Some are appointed for your physical care when you are without your biological parents. They provide food, shelter, and clothing. They even ensure your education and lead you to grow in the faith. Others may be your spiritual parents who teach you the Word of God, such as your pastor or Sunday school teacher. No matter their assignment, you must love and respect them dearly.

Hebrews 13:17

Be responsive to your pastoral leaders. Listen to their counsel.
They are alert to the condition of your lives and
work under the strict supervision of God.
Contribute to the joy of their leadership, not its drudgery.
Why would you want to make things harder for them?

My momma told me that I can lean on Jesus
When I'm falling down.
She said he'll pick me up when I'm low,
If he has to reach way down.

~CB

Princess—
Draw or place a picture of you and a family member in church.

CHAPTER 4
Prayer Time

Hi Moms, Dads, Guardians, and Teachers,

Isn't it awesome to know that God wants us to be in constant communication with him? Unlike humans, we will stop answering our phone when we don't feel up to talking. You would even think with all God has to do to maintain the universe, that surely, He is too busy to hear us or even to talk to us; but just the opposite, God wants us to teach our children to always pray. All throughout the day, teach them to make their requests known to Him. Teach them to speak the word back to God in faith. Tell them to speak to our Father from their hearts. They do not have to use speeches or copy off what they hear others say to God. This is why it is so important to teach our children the word.

Deuteronomy 6:7

Impress them on your children. Talk about them when you sit at home and when you walk along the road, when you lie down and when you get up.

PAPA'S LITTLE PRINCESS

Hi Princess,

What have you been doing today? Did you think about Me? I haven't heard from you today. These are some of the questions I may have in My heart to ask you. Answer as if you are talking only to Me, your heavenly father. Tell Me about your day and the different challenges you may have faced. While you are talking to Me, I am reminding you of the holy words I have already hidden in your heart. This is called prayer.

1 Thessalonians 5:17

… pray continually…

I really want you to know that I listen for your voice. You can even ask Me for things in line with My will, okay? The way to do this is to know what I have promised, so don't forget how important it is to learn of Me through the scriptures. As a child, you will get this teaching through those whom I have sent to be your guardians, parents, pastors, and teachers. You can also learn a lot as you learn how to read and understand the Holy Bible that I left on earth as your guide. Take time and talk to Me all through the day. I want you to listen very closely with your heart, because I will be speaking back to you in your spirit. Talk to me about your family, friends, and even your day-to-day stuff.

Dear God, I'm so happy you are there,
Just wanted to say a little prayer.
The time has come for me to sleep,
I pray dear Lord my soul you'll keep.
When I awake to see another day,
I pray, dear Lord, you'll lead the way.

Princess—
Write a prayer to Papa!

CHAPTER 5
The Girl in the Mirror

Hi Mom, Dads, Guardians, and Teachers,

I noticed when my granddaughter first saw herself in the mirror. She stood there for a while; I imagined she noticed her face was her own and not like any other she had seen. I believe she then started to see and compare herself with other faces and expressions. This is the moment, if not before, that you can begin to encourage your princess about her inner and outer beauty. She may notice herself or others being complimented about hair, clothes, or just overall appearance. Give close attention to how she responds to these comments, as it can be long-term damage done if she is not made to FEEL beautiful in her own skin while understanding that fearing the Lord is better. Appearances seem to dominate our world today. Many have made reconstructive, surgical changes to their original features to conform to one that has been complimented for this or that. This is lack of confidence and low self-esteem. You are empowered to build your daughters in this area, so be attentive to how they see themselves.

Proverbs 31:30

*Charm is deceptive, and beauty is fleeting;
but a woman who fears the Lord is to be praised.*

Beauty works from the inside out, and this means that the hidden person inside that you have reared will always show up eventually.

1 Peter 3:3-4

…What matters is not your outer appearance—the styling of your hair, the jewelry you wear, the cut of your clothes—but your inner disposition.

Psalm 139:14

I am fearfully and wonderfully made.

Good Morning Princess,

I noticed you looking at yourself in the mirror. You are now taking the time to see what you look like. Remember what I told you? I made you and you are beautiful! I put your height, weight, skin tone, and all just exactly how I wanted you to be. If you want to express your beauty, do it in a way that shows you are confident in who you are and how you look, not to draw the attention of others. Carry yourself gracefully in conversation and posture. Sit up straight, walk with your head held high! Speak with confidence and wisdom, and remember I am with you everywhere you go.

Psalm 139:14

I praise you because I am fearfully and wonderfully made;
your works are wonderful,
I know that full well.

Well, you need to know beauty is also in attitude. It doesn't matter if you have the most expensive or the most trendy clothes and shoes.

This is simply a covering of your flesh. Rather you should have a beautiful personality and win the hearts of others with your spirit of humility learned from your leaders and the Word of God.

1 Peter 3:3-4

Your beauty should not come from outward adornment, such as elaborate hairstyles and the wearing of gold jewelry or fine clothes. Rather, it should be that of your inner self, the unfading beauty of a gentle and quiet spirit, which is of great worth in God's sight.

So if you want to really be admired, then it is very important to be nice to everyone, even those who don't treat you as well as they should, and to obey your parents in the Lord.

Ephesians 6:1

Children, obey your parents in the Lord, for this is right.

Don't worry if you don't have the latest clothes or hairstyles like the other girls. Those things are just coverings. They become false covering for an outer appearance that is praised. If you begin to put your faith in them to cover you over My protection, My glory that surrounds you, My light that shines from within you, then it becomes like a god to you and is false. When JESUS, my Son, was born, he was only able to wear swaddling clothing, or in other words, he was wrapped in a cloth.

Luke 2:6-7

While they were there, the time came for her to give birth. She gave birth to a son, her firstborn. She wrapped him in a blanket and laid him in a manger, because there was no room in the hostel.

Mirror, mirror on the wall,
Whose the fairest of them All?
Not the one with bright eyes or smooth skin, right?
Not the one who wears name brand or colors so bright?
But it's the girl who is seen and not heard,
And is adorned with obedience of God's Holy Word.

CHAPTER 6
Play Time

Hi Moms, Dads, Guardians, and Teachers,

The Lord wants you to be concerned about the time when children are not in your presence. Since the earth houses natural spirits, they find it easy to influence such tender hearts. So He holds you responsible for protecting the eyes, ears, mouth, and the rest of the body of our daughters. God gave each parent full responsibility for even the atmosphere their children are in. Many things go sour for children when their protection is not around. The possibility of abduction, abuse, hearing bad words, being molested, developing bad habits, and other terrible things are higher than ever when you are not around. In fact, many have even told guardians they were hurt by others and their stories were not believed.

On another note, there will be some places little ones will have to be left, and you will have to prepare them for your absence. Places like schools, play grounds, and even dance lessons, where they are placed in the hands of other adults and in the room with other children. One way to prepare your child is to teach them how to get along with others, tell you what goes on when you are not around, and to respect adults.

Hi Princess,

It is time for you to start being around other people besides your family. You may already have some kids or adults you have met and either like or don't like being around. Most of the way you feel about others was learned from observation or will be taught by Mom and Dad.

Proverbs 22:6

*Start children off on the way they should go,
and even when they are old they will not turn from it.*

John 3:16

It is important to love everyone with my kind of love

Sometimes people do not behave nicely, but you have to learn to love everyone just as I do. However, this does not mean you are to be mistreated by anyone. You must do good to others. You must try to use words that will inspire, not use the language of demands or force. As you allow Me to love you, and you see how I treat you with mercy (not as you deserve) try to do the same. A soft answer turns away wrath.

Psalm 37:27

*Turn from evil and do good;
then you will dwell in the land forever.*

*My mom took me to school one day
And left me in the class
She said to me, "You're not alone
When you need the Lord, just ask"*

*Later, I said, "Teacher, teacher, Get the Lord for me"
She said, "Why princess, I'm here"
I said, "Yes, but I need Him now
to drive away this spirit of fear"*

*I said, "Teacher, teacher, Get the Lord for me"
She said, "You can call Him for yourself"
I said, "Oh, that's right, I sure can"
And He said, "Guess what, I never left"*

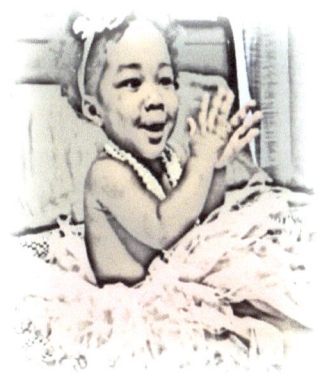 

www.ingramcontent.com/pod-product-compliance
Lightning Source LLC
Chambersburg PA
CBHW040356190426
43201CB00039B/34